How to Get an A Grade

in OCR Philosophy of Religion

Peter Baron

Published by Inducit Learning Ltd trading as PushMe Press

Mid Somerset House, Southover, Wells

Somerset BA5 1UH, United Kingdom

www.pushmepress.com

First published in 2014

ISBN: 978-1-909618-61-9

G571 & G581 specifications and past exam questions © OCR Examination Board, used with permission

All images © their respective owners

Contents

Helping you Get an A Grade 5

Introduction 7

What Are Exams For?..9

How to Analyse the Specification 17

How to Analyse Past Exam Questions............................39

How to Bring Specification and Past Questions Together ..55

What the Examiner Says 83

Helping you Get an A Grade

Effective learning involves reducing difficult topics into smaller, "bite-sized" chunks.

Every revision guide, card or coursebook from PushMe Press comes with its own website consisting of summaries, handouts, games, model essays, revision notes and more. Each website community is supported by the best teachers in the country.

At the end of each chapter you will see an **i-pu-sh** web link that you can type into your web browser along with a QR code that can be scanned by our free app.

These links will give you immediate access to the additional resources you need to "Get an A Grade" by providing you with the relevant information needed.

Getting an A Grade has never been easier.

Download our FREE How to Get an A Grade in Philosophy app for your phone or tablet and get up-to-date information that accompanies this book and the whole PushMe Press range.

http://philosophy.pushmepress.com/download

SAMPLE ESSAYS

You need to understand the difference between AO1 (analytical) and AO2 (evaluative) criteria which are used in marking your exam. You will find a discussion of these exam marking criteria attached to marked sample essays by scanning this code. Teachers also have added suggestions on how to improve these real answers. Essays are arranged by syllabus theme.

http://i-pu.sh/D2N45K33

EXTENDING (ALPHA POINTS)

Some analytical or evaluative points raise the quality of your answers. We call these "extending" points (for example, making a connection with another idea or a different philosopher). For a list of such extending points by topic, you can scan this code.

http://i-pu.sh/R9D10C90

Introduction

Perhaps a better title might have been "how to maximise your chances in Philosophy of Religion exams". What I have been trying to teach you with this book, the How to Write Essays book and the Coursebooks and Revision Guides is a method. The method is about doing philosophy and not regurgitating lines from a textbook. Indeed, you need to be aware that textbooks often work against you in the bid for an A grade. Why is this?

You need to learn thinking skills and practise a strategy. The thinking skills are not the heart of a textbook and the strategy isn't mentioned at all. In this book I will lay out the strategy and if you follow it, you will do what my students over the years have found: you will get the grade you really deserve, the one that reflects your true potential. The strategy is based on five principles, and each principle is carefully explained in this book. I have done a lot of the work for you. Your job now is to use it intelligently.

- **PRINCIPLE 1** - Understand the philosophy behind your exam.

- **PRINCIPLE 2** - Do a close analysis of the exam syllabus.

- **PRINCIPLE 3** - Do a close analysis of past questions.

- **PRINCIPLE 4** - Do a close analysis of the relationship between syllabus and questions.

- **PRINCIPLE 5** - Do a close analysis of the Chief Examiner's mark schemes and reports.

The first chapter and the final chapter are shared with my How to Get an A Grade in Ethics book. After all, they are both branches of philosophy and so they share certain principles of logical thought. However, I have changed the examples so that they apply specifically to Philosophy of Religion. Chapters 3 to 5 are specially written for this syllabus and contain the core of the analysis of the syllabus, past questions and potential future questions. If you follow the logic of this book, you will see that you need to pay especially close attention to chapter 5 where I bring past questions and potential future questions together. If you cover both there is not much more you can do.

Finally, I include throughout the book some ideas on how to revise effectively, both as an individual and as a group, including a number of class revision exercises.

What Are Exams For?

Is there a reason for exams, a philosophy behind the Philosophy of Religion you are doing?

The answer is "yes", and it helps if you understand the philosophy behind Philosophy, because in the end, if you become a philosopher and can show this in the exam, you should gain close to full marks.

The word philosophy means "a love of wisdom", and we gain wisdom by exercising a special type of thinking skill. The Greeks believed this skill was a foundational skill, because thinking well was a key to living well. So, we might ask, how do we "think well"?

I was encouraged recently to hear of a school which has a cookie club which meets at 4pm every week on a Thursday. The idea of the cookie club is to meet and debate - or if you like, to argue a case. Sometimes a member of staff, and sometimes a pupil comes with a case to defend, and everyone has to argue against the point of view that pupil is defending.

Something like this underlies the subject of philosophy. Philosophy is about presenting, arguing and then defending a case. So for example, Plato uses a method of dispute in his writing, called the Socratic method, where he puts words into the mouth of an adversary and then proceeds to dispute and disprove that opponent's case.

Of course this begs some questions.

WHAT DO I ACTUALLY BELIEVE ABOUT, SAY, GOD AND SCIENCE?

I attended a conference recently on Science and Religion. Part of the conference contained a debate between a well-known scientist and a leading theologian. The debate seemed to get stuck on one point: what is the place of a metaphysical view of the world when applied to science? In other words, at what point does science move into metaphysics, or begin to make assumptions which are essentially unprovable by any scientific method? It is easy to parrot the views of Richard Dawkins, for example. He has implied in interviews that to believe in God is irrational, and even that no intelligent person could believe in God. There are two things wrong with this view: first, that as an empirical fact many intelligent people do believe in God and second, that scientists slip in non-empirical statements all the time. For example, "the theory of the Big Bang" has at its heart a metaphor: there was no bang and it certainly wasn't big as there was nothing to compare it to at the beginning of time. The metaphor however encapsulates an essential truth about the theory: that something happened to propel an instant inflation where the universe was born (another metaphor) and then expanded very rapidly. And, here's a key fact, all the fragments of evidence we can glean from the solar system with our very powerful telescopes suggest that this theory best fits the facts.

Yet it begs philosophical questions. What caused the Big Bang? What existed beforehand? Could there be an eternal intelligence, a moral consciousness behind the universe?

In your A level, have the courage to present, and then own for yourself, good, strong, well-justified arguments in answer to such questions and you will be on the way to an A grade.

WHAT MAKES AN ARGUMENT WEAK?

A weak argument can really only be of two types. It can be logically unsound. And it can be factually unsound. Some arguments may present both weaknesses.

For example, consider this argument:

1. The world is either flat or square.

2. The world is not flat.

3. So the world must be square.

What is wrong with this? Well, it is false in two senses. First it commits a logical mistake - of restricting the options. It only gives us a choice of two possibilities, flat or square, when in fact there are many possible shapes, and the correct answer, the world is round, isn't given as a possibility.

Second, it is empirically or factually false. As a matter of fact, if I set off in my little sailing boat and head west (assuming I remember to navigate for the Panama Canal) I will eventually end up where I started. So I can attack the argument on two grounds, the logical and the factual, making clear what my two grounds are.

What about this argument about religious language:

1. Language is either analytic or synthetic.

2. Religious language is neither.

3. So religious language is meaningless.

What is wrong with this argument? It actually begs a question, or perhaps begs two questions. First of all, it suggests that language can only be of two types: analytical propositions such as "all bachelors are unmarried" where the truth is contained within the meaning of the term "bachelor", and synthetic statements such as "my Uncle John is a bachelor" which is either true or false depending on our finding his marriage certificate. But this excludes a whole section of human discourse, including poetic discourse, and talk about beauty and values and God.

Second, the conclusion doesn't follow. The conclusion is that language which is neither analytic nor synthetic is meaningless. But religious language and poetry are clearly meaningful within their own terms. We must also be wary of reductionism. Is human consciousness brain waves? Certainly. But is it just brain waves? Certainly not. Human consciousness is about perception, and perception is a lot more than brain waves. Indeed, scientists admit they are really a long way from understanding consciousness and the relationship between brain waves and what you are seeing right now. Consciousness cannot be reduced to brain waves and poetry cannot be reduced to words: to do so is **REDUCTIONISM**.

Sometimes the conclusions we come to simply don't follow - because the conclusion "religious language is meaningless" begs the question "what makes language meaningful"? We cannot just assume that the empiricists have got it right on this question: that is to fall into the trap of accepting a view uncritically, something we must try not to do.

WHAT MAKES AN ARGUMENT STRONG?

A strong argument proceeds by a logical form, from assumptions to conclusion. On the way the argument requires analysis and, if the question demands it, evaluation. Many students don't understand the difference between analysis and evaluation, so perhaps we can clarify this.

Analysis means that an argument proceeds by a process of reasoning. When we reason we substantiate (back up) the argument. This means we give justifications for a particular viewpoint. For example, we say that Kant argues that morality (and hence his moral argument) is produced by an a priori process of reasoning, because he sees the moral ought as applying universally, everywhere, and for all time. If this is the case, then he argues we cannot be subject to the realm of emotions or peer group pressure, because this would make the moral ought conditional on what people think or feel at any particular time.

Notice that in this argument I use the word "because" a number of times. I spell out the reasons for my reasoning. I also use a hypothetical statement, which starts with "if" and then continues with "then". The "if" here is indicating an underlying assumption, that we can divide the world up into two realms of thinking, what Kant calls the noumenal world (of pure ideas) and the phenomenal world (of experiences that we feel, see or touch).

If I were evaluating Kant and his moral argument rather than giving a Kantian analysis, then I might question this assumption. Is it a good way of looking at the world? Can there really be a pure realm of ideas in themselves? How does this differ from other worldviews?

HOW DO I PRACTISE STRENGTHENING ARGUMENTS?

I wrote a book last year with my colleague Brian Poxon called How to Write Philosophy Essays. In that book we describe a technique for writing essays. Here's a brief description of how this technique works.

Imagine I have an essay title like "'Miracles are unbelievable because they break natural laws.' Discuss." I need to practise presenting what we can call my thesis in the first line of the essay. The thesis is simply your statement of your line of reasoning on this particular question. For example, my thesis might be "Miracles are believable because, although they may break natural laws, they do not have to do so; they may simply be unusual events, and even if they do break natural laws, they are miracles because they reflect who God is rather than human ideas of what is possible".

This statement has the advantage of being relevant to this exact question and also clear. I can also reduce every paragraph to a one-sentence statement of the argument of that paragraph.

- **THESIS** - Miracles are believable because they depend on God's character, not on human ideas of scientific possibility.

- **PARAGRAPH 1** - The biologist Richard Dawkins argues that nothing is possible outside of a scientific probability which is determined by our understanding of natural laws.

- **PARAGRAPH 2** - Many events are outside scientific understanding. Give examples.

- **PARAGRAPH 3** - The miraculous can mean one of two things - the improbable or the impossible. Quote some other authors (eg Swinburne).

- **PARAGRAPH 4** - The biblical account of miracles sees them as signs which point to the nature of God - as Creator (Jesus walks on water showing creator power), and redeemer (Jesus heals people with words like "Go in faith" and "Your sins are forgiven" - so showing how to buy us back/redeem from death).

- **CONCLUSION** - Judging miracles by scientific criteria is misguided, as miracles should be judged against the probability or otherwise of the existence of God.

So, try to sketch out a thesis, practise this technique, and then try saying something interesting, surprising even, which of course must be fully justified. This is how you maximise chances of an A grade.

WHY DO DEFINITIONS MATTER SO MUCH?

In Philosophy of Religion there is technical vocabulary which must be used correctly. But we need to be aware that the task of philosophy is also to indicate ambiguities in key words, how they are used differently in different contexts and how the meaning is not necessarily clear-cut or fixed.

I was listening to a debate on Question Time recently and it became clear to me that two sides of this debate were actually talking about a different thing. The subject was gay marriage. On one side, the definition of marriage meant something like "a relationship where two people are fully committed to one another". No mention of sexual relations here.

On the other side, the definition was something like this: "marriage is a lifelong commitment between a man and a woman where heterosexual sex is the natural expression, and children the natural fruit, of such a lifelong commitment". Notice that this definition includes both sex and the possibility of children.

I think the chairman of this debate, David Dimbleby, should have pointed out that people were talking about two different things. The question is, which is the correct definition, or the most useful definition? Clearly the second is the traditional view of marriage, whereby not having sexual relations is a ground for divorce or annulment of the marriage. Once we have established we are talking about different things we can then decide what we think.

Does it matter that the definition of marriage is changing? Should marriage necessarily include some idea of sexual relations if it doesn't; could I marry someone who remains my best friend, who I never even touch? If marriage includes some idea of sexual relations, how do we define sexual relations between two men?

All this helps to clarify the debate - and this is the task of philosophy. For philosophy has at its heart a philosophy of argument - of clarification, reasoning and conclusions which make sense. To argue effectively we cannot help defining and clarifying our terms, and indicating possible ambiguities in their use. The examiner's reports, analysed in the final chapter, repeatedly emphasise that a failure to grasp key terms is a major reason why candidates don't get A grades.

How to Analyse the Specification

Students can sometimes be surprised by questions set in the exam. However, there never should be any element of surprise, as the specifications (syllabuses) lay down exactly what you can expect in the exam. Therefore surprise can only come because there is an area of the specification we failed to notice, or failed to cover adequately. A-grade technique involves:

- Examining the specification, paying close attention to specific authors mentioned.

- Relating past questions to the specification to see how the examiner interprets the specification, which may be ambiguous in places.

In this section we will analyse the four specifications, before matching the specification to past questions in a later chapter.

AS PHILOSOPHY OF RELIGION (OCR G571)

Ancient Greek influences on Philosophy of Religion

Candidates are expected to have a basic knowledge of the thinking of Plato and Aristotle; they will not be expected to have first-hand knowledge of the texts. They should be able to highlight the strengths and weaknesses in the thinking of Plato and Aristotle in the areas specified below.

Plato: The Analogy of the Cave

▸ **The Republic VII. 514A-521B**

Candidates should be able to demonstrate knowledge and understanding of what might be represented in the Analogy of the Cave by:

- The prisoners

- The shadows

- The cave itself

- The outside world

- The sun

- The journey out of the cave and the return to the prisoners

Candidates should be able to discuss critically the validity of the points being made in this analogy.

▸ Plato: The concept of the Forms; the Form of the Good

Candidates should understand what Plato meant by "Forms" and be able to demonstrate knowledge and understanding of:

- The relationship between concepts and phenomena

- The concept of "Ideals"

- The relationship between the Form of the Good and the other Forms

Candidates should be able to discuss critically the validity of the above points.

Aristotle: Ideas about cause and purpose in relation to God (Metaphysics Book 12)

Candidates should be able to demonstrate knowledge and understanding of:

- Aristotle's understanding of material, efficient, formal and final cause

- Aristotle's concept of the Prime Mover

Candidates should be able to discuss critically the validity of the above points.

Judaeo-Christian influences on Philosophy of Religion

Candidates should be familiar with biblical texts to exemplify the topics below. There are no prescribed texts.

▸ The concept of God as creator

Candidates should be able to demonstrate knowledge and understanding of:

- The way the Bible presents God as involved with his creation

- The imagery of God as a craftsman

- The concepts of omnipotence, omniscience and omnipresence

- The concept of "creatio ex nihilo"

Candidates should be able to:

- Compare this view with Aristotle's Prime Mover

- Discuss whether, if God created the universe, God is therefore responsible for everything that happens in it

Candidates should be able to discuss these areas in a critical manner.

▸ The goodness of God

Candidates should be able to demonstrate knowledge and understanding of:

- The ways in which the God of the Bible is seen as morally perfect and the source of human ethics

- The concept of God as lawgiver and as judge

Candidates should be able to:

- Consider whether, in a biblical context, God commands things because they are good or whether things are good because God commands them

Candidates should be able to discuss these areas in a critical manner.

▸ Traditional arguments for the existence of God

The ontological argument from Anselm and Descartes; challenges from Gaunilo and Kant.

Candidates should be able to demonstrate knowledge and understanding of:

- The ontological argument from Anselm and Descartes

- Challenges to it from Gaunilo and Kant

- Anselm's understanding of God - his understanding of the differences between contingent and necessary existence

- Descartes' understanding of existence as a perfection which God cannot lack

- Gaunilo's analogy of the island in On Behalf of the Fool

Candidates should be able to discuss these areas in a critical manner.

▸ **The cosmological argument from Aquinas and Copleston; challenges from Hume and Russell**

Candidates should be able to demonstrate knowledge and understanding of:

- The cosmological argument from Aquinas and Copleston

- The arguments put forward by Copleston in the 1948 radio debate with Russell and Russell's counter-arguments

- Hume's criticisms of the cosmological argument

Candidates should be able to discuss critically these views and their strengths and weaknesses.

▸ **The teleological argument from Aquinas and Paley; challenges from Hume, Mill and Darwin**

Candidates should be able to demonstrate knowledge and understanding of:

- The teleological argument from Aquinas and Paley

- The challenges to it from Hume, Mill and Darwinism

Candidates should be able to discuss critically these views and their strengths and weaknesses.

▸ **The moral argument from Kant: psychological challenges from Freud**

- The moral argument from Kant, including his concept of the "summum bonum" and his inferences about innate moral awareness

- Psychological challenges from Freud to the moral argument; his view that moral awareness comes from sources other than God

Candidates should be able to discuss critically these views and their strengths and weaknesses.

Challenges to religious belief

▸ **The problem of evil**

Candidates should be able to demonstrate knowledge and understanding of:

- The problem of evil: the classic theodicies of Augustine and Irenaeus

- The nature of the problem of evil and the possible differences between natural and moral evil

- How each theodicy understands the responsibility of God for the existence of evil in the world

- The origins of evil and the role of human free will

Candidates should be able to discuss critically these approaches and their strengths and weaknesses.

▶ Religion and science

Candidates should be able to demonstrate knowledge and understanding of:

- Scientific and philosophical views on the creation of the universe; particularly the debate between Creationism and the Big Bang theory

- Darwinism and various developments of evolutionary theory

- "Intelligent design" and "irreducible complexity"

- Religious responses to challenges posed by scientific views

Candidates should be able to discuss critically these views and their strengths and weaknesses.

Technical language in the syllabus

The following phrases or technical terms occur in the syllabus (in order of appearance below). They represent a minimum checklist of technical vocabulary. These terms, and only these terms, may appear in an exam question, and so you will be hampered in your answer if you don't understand how they are used (and any ambiguity or difference in use by philosophers).

- The Form of the Good

- Ideals

- Phenomena

- Material, efficient, formal and final cause

- Prime Mover

- Omnipotence

- Omniscience

- Omnipresence

- Creatio ex nihilo

- Cosmological argument

- Teleological argument

- Moral argument

- Summum bonum

- Theodicy

- Creationism

- Big Bang theory

- Intelligent design

- Irreducible complexity

Authors mentioned

The following authors are listed in the syllabus, and so they should be carefully studied, with summary sheets of their views produced (the area of the syllabus to which each relates can be cross-referenced above). Also note that the need to critically consider these views means that some countervailing view also needs to be assessed. To do this you will need to specify some authors who do not agree with the views cited by the above.

- Plato (Analogy of the Cave)

- Aristotle (Metaphysics Book 12)

- Anselm (ontological argument)

- Descartes

- Gaunilo

- Kant (criticisms of the ontological argument)

- Aquinas (cosmological argument)

- Copleston

- Russell (radio debate with Copleston)

- Hume (criticisms of the cosmological argument)

- Aquinas (second appearance, this time the teleological argument)

- Paley

- Hume (criticisms of the teleological argument)

- Mill (criticisms)

- Darwin

- Kant (second appearance, this time the moral argument)

- Freud (psychological challenges)

- Augustine (free will)

- Irenaeus

- Darwin (religion and science debate)

The first thing we can note from this list is that there are 20 authors whose arguments we need to clarify. There is clearly potential for confusion here, and a good student needs to think carefully about the differences between these various arguments. Then there are additional authors that need to be added, for example, Richard Dawkins is not on the syllabus as a named author, but as a contemporary exponent of evolutionary design, he will need to be studied (and perhaps a good student will study him alongside Darwin to see how he developed Darwin's insights, with the theory of memes and the origin of conscience through the altruistic or "selfish" gene - which are actually the same thing, paradoxically, as it is the self-promoting gene which produces the requirement to co-operate together, and so produces over time the genetic basis for altruism or sense of sympathy and compassion for others).

There are also a number of texts which need to be studied. It is worth reading them for yourself, even though the syllabus states "the candidate will not be expected to have first-hand knowledge of the texts themselves", because the best way to gain full understanding is always to return to the original source and then compare that with what commentators say. Aristotle's Metaphysics 12 is mentioned, as is Plato's Cave Analogy (Book VII, The Republic). The radio debate between Copleston and Russell needs to be studied carefully. Who do you think won it by producing the strongest argument for or against the cosmological argument? Be aware too that many of these arguments may be a number of different arguments - for example, Anselm produced at least two versions of the ontological argument for God's existence.

Ambiguities in the syllabus

In this syllabus there are a number of places where teacher and student have to fill in the gaps. A diligent student needs to keep an eye on these gaps: it is too easy for a teacher to run out of time and leave a gap unfilled. The difference between the A-grade student and a lesser-grade student is often that the A-grade student is not too teacher dependent, but takes responsibility for their own understanding and interpretation of the syllabus, so making sure any gaps are filled whether they are covered in class or not.

Here's my list of gaps that need to be filled:

> "Biblical texts on the concept of God as creator and the goodness of God."

There are no set texts, meaning passages from the Bible, so we need to find some, such as Genesis 1-2, Exodus 34: 1-6.

> "Consider whether, in a Biblical context, God commands things because they are good or whether things are good because God commands them."

This is a statement of "Euthyphro's Dilemma" first argued by Plato in a fictitious discussion between Euthyphro and Socrates. You could look at the Ten Commandments for example, and see how these are given in the context of a revelation of the character of God (Exodus 20-34). Some would argue that the dilemma is itself a fallacy because it restricts the options to two: morality comes from God's words (commands) or from reason, whereas it could be argued in the context of Exodus 34 that the Ten Commandments are given because God is revealed as the "God of steadfast love and faithfulness" - there is a difference, by analogy, between a parent saying "do this because I say so" (command), and "do this because I love you and want the best for you". But this third option isn't considered by Euthyphro's Dilemma, and so it closes off the most plausible biblical reason for the commands of God.

"The origins of evil" (Problem of Evil section)

This is a huge area of controversy which could embrace psychological theories such as behaviourism, which suggests that we are conditioned by our environment to behave "evilly", to psychological theories of the origin of action in childhood (Freud, Piaget), to genetic influences. Because it is open-ended it is up to you to take whatever line you like on the issue of where evil comes from, but to ground your views in scholarship, and find your own authors to add to the above list.

You can continue this analysis of ambiguities for yourself: the important point is that every A-grade student should do a close analysis of the syllabus and then continue to refer back and use the syllabus as the starting point. Many of these sections have sufficient leeway to make the question "are we departing from the syllabus?" (which I have heard teachers use) a fairly meaningless one. To some extent the syllabus is determined by you, and how you relate interconnected ideas to the main themes outlined above.

A2 PHILOSOPHY OF RELIGION (OCR G581)

Although the A2 syllabus appears on the face of it to be shorter, it includes some complex terminology and a series of quite challenging philosophical ideas. So again, a careful analysis of technical vocabulary, authors mentioned and ambiguities will help us clarify what is required of the A-grade student.

Religious language

Candidates should be able to demonstrate knowledge and understanding of:

- Religious language - uses and purpose

- The via negativa (Apophatic Way)

- The verification and falsification principles

- Different views on the meaningfulness of religious language

- The uses of symbol, analogy and myth to express human understanding of God

- The views of the Vienna Circle, AJ Ayer, Anthony Flew, Ludwig Wittgenstein and Paul Tillich on religious language

Candidates should be able to discuss these areas critically and their strengths and weaknesses.

Religious experience

Candidates should be able to demonstrate knowledge and understanding of the following in relation to God and religious belief:

- Arguments from religious experience from William James

- The aims and main conclusions drawn by William James in The Varieties of Religious Experience

- The following different forms of religious experience:

  - Visions

  - Voices

  - "Numinous" experience

  - Conversion experience

  - Corporate religious experience

  - The concept of revelation through sacred writings

Candidates should be able to discuss these areas critically and their strengths and weaknesses.

Miracle

A study of how God might interact with humanity, by looking at the concept of miracle.

Candidates should be able to demonstrate knowledge and understanding of:

- Different definitions of miracle, including an understanding of Hume

- The biblical concept of miracle and the issues this raises about God's activity in the world

- The concept of miracle, and criticisms made by Hume and Wiles

- The implications of the concept of miracle for the problem of evil

Candidates should be able to discuss whether modern people can be expected to believe in miracles, and whether miracles suggest an arbitrary or partisan God. Candidates should be able to discuss these areas critically and their strengths and weaknesses.

Attributes

▸ Nature of God

Candidates should be able to demonstrate knowledge and understanding of:

- God as eternal, omniscient, omnipotent and omnibenevolent - and the philosophical problems arising from these concepts

- The views of Boethius in his discussion of eternity and God's foreknowledge in Book 5 of The Consolations of Philosophy

- The question as to whether or not a good God should reward and punish

Candidates should be able to discuss these areas critically and their strengths and weaknesses.

Life and death; the soul

▸ Life and death

Candidates should be able to demonstrate knowledge and understanding of:

- Distinctions between body and soul, as expressed in the thinking of Plato, Aristotle, John Hick and Richard Dawkins

- Other concepts of the body/soul distinction

- Different views of life after death: resurrection and reincarnation

- Questions surrounding the nature of disembodied existence

- The relationship between the afterlife and the problem of evil

Candidates should be able to discuss these areas critically and their strengths and weaknesses.

Technical language in the syllabus

- Via negativa

- Apophatic Way

- Verification principle

- Falsification principle

- Symbol

- Analogy

- Myth

- Numinous religious experience

- Corporate religious experience

- Miracle

- Omnipotent

- Omniscient

- Omnibenevolent

- Foreknowledge

- Soul

- Resurrection

- Reincarnation

Again we need to stress that this is a minimum list - but it represents terms which could appear in the actual exam question, and for this reason they must be throughly learned and understood. A good technique for an opening paragraph is to clarify and define your terms, making sure you indicate ambiguities within them. For example, many students assume that the term "resurrection" is clear from the biblical accounts. But this is far from the case. Jesus appears as a physical body and yet he walks through closed doors and isn't recognised by his followers on the road to Emmaus. St Paul says we are "raised imperishable" with a "spiritual body" (1 Corinthians 15), but what does he mean by a "spiritual body"? Is it a replica of our old body, and if so, our old body at what state of existence (I wouldn't want to live eternally with a decrepit athritic body)? If it's not an exact replica, how is the resurrection body different? Simply outlining some of these difficulties allows us to proceed in an A-grade direction.

Authors mentioned

- AJ Ayer

- Anthony Flew

- Ludwig Wittgenstein

- Paul Tillich

- William James (Varieties of Religious Experience)

- David Hume

- Maurice Wiles

- Boethius (Consolations of Philosophy Book V)

- Plato (Life after Death)

- Aristotle

- John Hick

- Richard Dawkins

There are 12 authors specifically mentioned and one key text (Boethius). However, there are a number of authors a good student would be unwise to neglect. For example, Richard Swinburne has written extensively on a number of issues here, not least life after death. Anthony Flew has written not just on religious language (where he is mentioned and so could appear in an actual question), but also on miracles and life after death. I would always encourage students to read some original sources and to quote the authors themselves.

Ambiguities

There are always gaps to fill and interpretations to make of any syllabus. Here's a short list of the ones in the A2 Philosophy of Religion syllabus.

"Religious language - uses and purpose."

What exactly are the "uses" of religious language? (Worship, prayer, private meditation, parables, credal statements.)

"The concept of revelation through sacred writings."

The syllabus deliberately leaves this ambiguous because we can choose any religion to illustrate the idea of revelation, and different religions of the world take very different views on this. Assuming for the moment that we take Christianity as our religion, there are a number of different views of the status of the Bible. For example, you might read the Chicago statement on Biblical Inerrancy to find a contemporary justification for taking the Bible as the inerrant word of God: the statement was written by American academics as recently as 1967. This could then be contrasted with liberal views of revelation, using insights from the religious language section (about how myth works, for example). Many candidates fail to discuss non-propositional forms of revelation.

"The biblical concept of miracle."

Again, there is a central ambiguity here, not clarified by the syllabus. What is the biblical concept of miracle? Theologians take different views on this. What does seem true, however, is that the Bible doesn't take the definition of miracle that philosophers do. Philosophers tend to take a scientific view of miracle, as "an event which breaks natural law", whereas theologians tend to argue from the perspective of John's Gospel, that miracles are signs which tell us something about the nature of the Messiah (in the New Testament) or Yahweh (in the Hebrew Scriptures). These two ideas are sufficiently different to suggest that the term itself is ambiguous, and needs to be clarified against the worldview of 2,000 years ago.

"Whether or not a good God should reward or punish."

This begs the question whether goodness includes some idea of justice (and a complete intolerance of sin inherent in the idea of holiness). The ideas of "reward" and "punishment" are also in need of careful treatment. Compare for example the idea of those who fail to attend to the needs of the poor in Matthew 25 "as if serving Christ himself" as the basis of judgement and casting into eternal fire, with the idea in John's Gospel that "who believes in the Son has life, but he who does not believe has not life, and the wrath of God rests upon him". This seems to suggest that we are justified by belief (the Evangelical Protestant view that we are justified by faith alone) and punished accordingly. This appears to contradict the idea in Matthew 25, the Parable of the Sheep and the Goats, that the basis of punishment is our actions on earth and whether we care for those less fortunate than ourselves in an appropriate way.

"Resurrection and reincarnation."

Here are two "big ideas". Unfortunately both are ambiguous. The idea of reincarnation operates differently in the Buddhist system of thought (and maybe in varieties of Buddhist thinking) than in Hindu thinking. Buddhists refer to "no-self" rather than different stages of reincarnated being (as in Hinduism). Thus the ambiguity of the term needs to be carefully addressed and critically evaluated. An A-grade candidate will never assume we (or the syllabus itself) knows what we are talking about, especially when what we are talking about, once defined, so determines the nature of our analysis.

How to Analyse Past Exam Questions

Past exam questions give us critical clues as to how the examiner interprets the specification. As indicated in the previous chapter, the specification is ambiguous in several areas, and open to interpretation. What is certain is that no technical term or author will be mentioned in an exam question which isn't already mentioned in the syllabus.

The best approach to maximising A-grade potential is to study carefully the trends in the questions, to examine which have been set before, and then relate them to the syllabus. Any areas that have never been examined before, or not for some time, are more likely to occur in the next paper set, as examiners have to range their questions across the whole syllabus and not stick to areas that may be easier to set questions on.

Over the page is a table giving all AS Philosophy of Religion questions since 2010. These are then discussed further in a subsequent chapter where I suggest potential future questions (marked there with a star).

AS PHILOSOPHY OF RELIGION (OCR G571)

At AS level the questions are presented in two parts, with part a being worth 25 marks and part b ten marks. The marks roughly translate to the number of minutes you have to spend on each. So it is essential to practise writing essays in class time, first of all with some sort of plan, and then using memory alone.

	PLATO/ARISTOTLE	GOD OF CLASSICAL THEISM	COSMOLOGICAL ARGUMENT	TELEOLOGICAL ARGUMENT
Jan 2010	a. Explain the concept of Ideals in Plato's writing b. "Ideals are an illusion; we can only experience what is real." Discuss	a. Explain the concept of "creatio ex nihilo" b. "Nothing comes from nothing." Discuss		a. Explain Mill's challenge to the teleological argument b. Evaluate the claim that the universe has too many flaws for it to be designed
June 2010		a. Compare the concept of Prime Mover with that of God as a craftsman b. "Utilitarianism can lead to wrong moral decisions." Discuss		
Jan 2011		a. Explain what it means to say God is good b. To what extent are things only good because God commands them?		
June 2011	a. Explain Aristotle's understanding of the four causes b. "Aristotle's four causes fail as a description of the real world." Discuss		a. Explain Hume's criticisms of the cosmological argument b. To what extent was Hume successful in his criticisms of the cosmological argument?	a. Explain Paley's argument for the existence of God b. "The universe has no purpose." Discuss

40

	MORAL ARGUMENT	ONTOLOGICAL ARGUMENT	PROBLEM OF EVIL	SCIENCE & RELIGION
Jan 2010				a. Explain Darwinism and evolutionary theory b. "The universe is too complex for evolutionary theory to explain it." Discuss
June 2010	a. Explain Freud's view that moral awareness comes from sources other than God b. "War should not be allowed even as a last resort." Discuss	a. Explain Anselm's ontological argument b. "It is pointless to deny the logical necessity of the existence of God." Discuss		a. Explain the concept of irreducible complexity b. "There is no evidence of intelligent design in the universe." Discuss
Jan 2011	a. Explain what Kant means by "summum bonum" b. "The existence of morality is not evidence for the existence of God." Discuss		a. Explain the nature of the problem of evil b. "Moral evil may be the fault of humanity but moral evil is God's fault." Discuss	a. Explain why some creationists do not believe in the Big Bang theory b. "Scientists are the only ones who can explain why the universe is here." Discuss
June 2011			a. Explain the Irenaean theodicy b. To what extent can evil be said simply to be a test?	

	PLATO/ARISTOTLE	GOD OF CLASSICAL THEISM	COSMOLOGICAL ARGUMENT	TELEOLOGICAL ARGUMENT
Jan 2012	a. Explain how Kant challenged the ontological argument b. To what extent was Kant successful in his challenge to the ontological argument?	a. Explain biblical beliefs about the attributes of God b. "The Bible is too inconsistent to be used for moral teachings." Discuss	a. Explain the arguments put forward by Coplestone in his radio debate with Russell b. How far was Russell successful in countering Coplestone's arguments in the radio debate?	
June 2012	a. Explain the relationship between Plato's Form of the Good and other Forms b. "The Forms teach us nothing about the physical world." Discuss		a. Explain Aristotle's concept of the Prime Mover b. "An accidental universe is as likely as a created one." Discuss	
Jan 2013	a. Explain Plato's Analogy of the Cave b. "Plato is wrong to say that most people live in the shadow world." Discuss			a. Explain Mill's criticisms of the design argument b. "The teleological argument has successfully survived all criticisms." Discuss
May 2013		a. Explain what is meant by "creatio ex nihilo" b. "God should not judge us as he is responsible for the way we are." Discuss		

	MORAL ARGUMENT	ONTOLOGICAL ARGUMENT	PROBLEM OF EVIL	SCIENCE & RELIGION
Jan 2012				a. Compare scientific and philosophical views on the creation of the universe b. Evaluate the view that science can only explain how and not why the universe exists
June 2012	a. Explain Kant's moral argument for the existence of God b. "Morality has nothing to do with the existence of God." Discuss		a. Explain the theodicies of both Augustine and Irenaeus b. "There is too much evil in the world for there to be a God." Discuss	See also cosmological argument question
Jan 2013	a. Explain Freud's views on the source of moral awareness b. "Only God can be the source of moral awareness." Discuss			a. Explain the theory of evolution b. "God is the only explanation for the existence of life." Discuss
May 2013		a. Explain Descartes' version of the ontological argument b. "Descartes has proved that a perfect God exists." Discuss	a. Explain the theodicies of both Augustine and Irenaeus b. "There is too much evil in the world for there to be a God." Discuss	a. Explain what is meant by intelligent design b. "The intelligent design argument makes no sense." Discuss

The two parts also relate to different skills. There is no point wasting time in part a questions evaluating the plausibility of some theory or view when the question title only ever asks you to explain some theory or viewpoint, or on occasion to compare two viewpoints. The idea of comparison here involves lining two things up against each other, as you might compare two cars and observe differences between them: it does not mean you state which view you think is superior to the other. This would be an evaluation skill and you are never required to evaluate at part a of a question, and so you will simply lose time if you do, and gain no credit.

- **REVISION TIP** - Read through each other's work and be ruthless about underlining in red any deviation from the question set, and any use of evaluative language in part a questions. This will help you to really understand the difference between analysis and evaluation, and between comparing and critically comparing.

Spot the gaps

With eight topic areas there are sometimes up to three gaps before the examiner chooses to set a question again on a particular area. It is important also to look at possible questions that have not yet been set on a particular area. This is the subject of the next chapter.

Wording of the questions

The wording of part a questions only contains two command words: "explain" and "compare". Notice that in part a questions you will only be asked to explain rather than evaluate. So, again, we need to pay close attention to the specification and try putting the word "explain" in front of each subsection of the specification, or if there are two elements within an area of the specification, to compare them.

Which areas might we be expected to compare (a command word only used twice in essay titles since 2009)?

- Science v. religion on the origins of the universe (Jan 2012)

- Prime Mover v. God as craftsman (Jan 2010)

- Aristotle's Prime Mover v. God as Creator ex nihilo

- Descartes' and Anselm's versions of the ontological argument

- Copleston's and Russell's view of the cosmological argument

- Kant's and Freud's view of the origin of moral awareness

- The theodicy of Irenaeus and Augustine

- **REVISION TIP** - Try making up tables to compare these different views. The table could have sub-categories down the left-hand side, eg on science v. religion. The sub-categories might be: explanation, issues arising, problems/weaknesses with the view, strengths of the view. An issue here might be whether the two views, of science and religion for example, on creation can be reconciled, or the fact that there are a variety of religious views which need to be considered.

Part b questions

These ask you to evaluate a particular viewpoint. Most part b questions are statement followed by "Discuss". There is no substitute for practising writing an answer in 10 minutes, which leaves time for only two or three paragraphs. It is important to launch straight into your answer and to work out before you start writing what your thesis (your argument in one line) is going to be. This will require the skill of clear thinking and writing if you are going to obtain the full ten marks in part b.

In your discussion remember to unpack the key word or words in the statement you are asked to discuss. For example, if we are asked to evaluate whether Kant is successful in his criticisms of the ontological argument (Jan 2012), we need to unpack what "successful" means here. And if we are asked to consider whether the Bible is too "inconsistent" (Jan 2012) we need to discuss what this word "consistent" might mean, and whether the concept of consistency is appropriate for a mythological biblical worldview which produces a developing theology of God over 2,500 years and 66 books which make up the Old and New Testaments.

- **REVISION TIP** - Part b questions, worth 10 marks each, express an issue underlying that section of the syllabus. For example, with Plato's idea of the Forms, the issue is whether this is an adequate view of reality, whether reality is beyond human understanding or just reducible to what we observe. So practise making up your own part b questions, as statements with the word "Discuss" after them, which go to the heart of the issues philosophers are debating on the different syllabus areas.

- **REVISION TIP** - The examiner repeatedly stresses that candidates spend too long on part b questions (worth only 10 out of the total available of 35 marks) and not long enough on part a questions (worth 25/35). You must practise explaining more fully (and reflectively, really going to the heart of what key ideas mean and where they come from) in part a, and evaluating succinctly in part b.

A2 PHILOSOPHY OF RELIGION (OCR G581)

At A2 there are no part a and b questions, so analysis and evaluation can intertwine seamlessly in your analysis. The key syllabus areas are:

- Religious language

- Religious experience

- Miracles

- Attributes of God

- Life and death

But notice that theories of revelation come in the religious experience section of the syllabus, where a question may ask how God can reveal himself through sacred writings.

	RELIGIOUS LANGUAGE	RELIGIOUS EXPERIENCE
Jan 2010	4.Critically assess the views of Paul Tillich on religious language	
June 2010	1.Evaluate the claim that analogy can successfully be used to express the human understanding of God	3.Critically assess, with reference to William James, the argument from religious experience
Jan 2011	1.To what extent can God reveal himself through sacred writings? 2.Critically compare the use of myth with the use of analogy to express the human understanding of God	
June 2011	1.Critically assess the claim that religious language is meaningless	4."Visions are not caused by God but can be explained by science." Discuss
Jan 2012	3."The falsification principle presents no real challenge to religious belief." Discuss	1."Corporate religious experiences prove the existence of God." Discuss
June 2012	1.Critically assess Wittgenstein's belief that language games allow religious statements to have meaning	2."Conversion experiences are the strongest evidence for the existence of God." Discuss
Jan 2013	1.To what extent is the via negativa the only way to talk about God?	2.Critically assess the aims and conclusions of William James' The Varieties of Religious Experience'
June 2013	1."Symbolic language is the best way to talk about God." Discuss	

48

	MIRACLE	ATTRIBUTES OF GOD	LIFE & DEATH
Jan 2010	2."A belief in miracles leads to the concept of a God who favours some but not all of his creation." Discuss	1.Critically assess the philosophical problems raised by the belief that God is omniscient	3.Evaluate the claim that there can be no disembodied existence after death
June 2010		2."Boethius was successful in his argument that God rewards and punishes justly." Discuss	4.To what extent is belief in an afterlife necessary for resolving problems raised by the existence of evil?
Jan 2011	4.Evaluate Hume's claim that miracles are the least likely of events		3."Resurrection is more likely to be true than reincarnation." Discuss
June 2011		3.Critically assess the problems for believers who say that God is omniscient	2.Evaluate the claim that the soul is distinct from the body
Jan 2012	2.Critically assess the view that the concept of miracle is inconsistent with the belief in a benevolent God	4.Assess the claim that the universe shows no evidence of the existence of a benevolent God	
June 2012		3.Evaluate the philosophical problems raised by the belief that God is eternal	4.Critically compare Aristotle's and Richard Dawkins' views on body and soul identity
Jan 2013		3.Critically assess the philosophical problems raised by believing in an omnibenevolent God	4."The concept of embodied existence after death is incoherent." Discuss
June 2013	4.Critically assess Wiles' view on miracles	2.To what extent does Boethius succeed in proving that the Christian God is just?	3."The existence of evil cannot be justified if there is no life after death." Discuss

Spot the gaps

Because the syllabus has only five sections it is important to analyse questions set within each syllabus area. However, it does seem that when one area is omitted (as it has to be each year with four questions set) then it is almost guaranteed to be examined upon next time. On this basis, it seemed more likely (though of course not certain) that in June 2013 the exam would include a question on miracles. And indeed, this proved to be the case, with a question on Wiles' view of miracles.

In order to get some idea of what question the examiner is likely to set on miracles, I would then analyse the twist given to each question in past years and then compare this with the twists suggested by the syllabus.

Jan 2010

✓ Miracles and God's partiality

June 2010

✓ No question

Jan 2011

✓ Hume's view evaluated

June 2011

✓ No question

Jan 2012

✓ Miracles and God's benevolence

June 2013

✓ Wiles' concept of miracle (see my prediction below)

What questions does this leave out, which have not been examined before on miracles? (That's not to suggest that we neglect past questions in our revision, of course.) We arrive at the following list:

1. The biblical concept of miracle, linked to God's activity in the word. I would expect a question asking us to consider whether we can expect God's activity to be the same as that described in the Bible, or whether these ideas of miracles we find in the Bible are unique to the biblical worldview, and why.

2. Criticisms of the concept of miracle raised by Maurice Wiles. This was my prediction for June 2013, and see above - it appeared as expected.

3. A question linking miracles to the problem of evil and the character of God - for example, "it is immoral for an omnipotent God to allow natural evil to persist".

4. A question asking whether modern people can possibly believe in miracles, such as "miracles are unbelievable in a scientific age" or "miracles only make sense within a pre-modern worldview".

5. A question with the phrase "critically compare", such as "critically compare the view of miracles taken by Hume and Wiles".

We will continue this analysis in the next chapter, where you should pay close attention to the twists, as I will call them, which I suggest the examiner may give to a question on a specific syllabus area.

Wording of questions

The wordings of all A2 questions have a strong evaluative element within them. In fact the range of words used in exam questions is narrow.

"Critically assess" or "critically compare" occurred 10/24 times in our survey of questions from 2010 to 2012, meaning to weigh up arguments for this viewpoint and criticisms of the viewpoint, and crucially, then say which you think are valid or invalid and why (notice you are always supposed to come sort of firm conclusion to assess for an A grade. It is **NEVER** sufficient to say "there are strong arguments on both sides and so it ends up being a question of belief". Philosophy is always about developing a critical courage to come down in favour of one view or another, with reasons). As "critically compare" has only come as a command phrase once, it might be worth thinking which views could be compared within the syllabus. An obvious example is Hume's and Wiles' view of miracles.

- **REVISION TIP** - The more specific you make your revision, the more useful it will be. For example, if you carefully revise the biblical view of miracles and set it alongside that of Hume and Wiles, and learn some quotes for each view, then this detailed knowledge can be used for any question on miracles. Whereas if you only revise general arguments, you will be caught out when the examiner asks a question naming a specific philosopher listed in the syllabus.

"Discuss" is used 7/24 times in our survey. Of course, to discuss means to evaluate and to analyse but a statement with "discuss" after it is more obviously biased one way or another. Illustrating this again from miracles, the statement "miracles are unbelievable" is obviously biased against the evidence for the miraculous, and will involve a discussion of both the concept of "miracle" and the idea of what it means to be "believable".

- **REVISION TIP** - Always practise unpacking key terms in an essay question, and do so critically. For example, the idea of miracle is ambiguous between "against natural law" and "improbable event" and it is only the former definition which offends against a scientific view. Science can handle improbability (such as the odd person has survived falling out of an aircraft at 10,000 feet, due to snowdrifts or a strong updraught) but science cannot accept impossibility (such as Jesus walking on water).

"Evaluate" is used 5/24 times. Evaluate means to consider what is good or bad about a particular view, what is valid or invalid in the argument, or what is strong or weak about an argument. Evaluation can take place at different stages of the argument, and close attention should be paid to these different stages. For example, we can evaluate **DEFINITIONS** as ambiguous or clear, we can evaluate **ASSUMPTIONS** as valid or invalid, and we can evaluate **ARGUMENTS** as strong or weak and **CONCLUSIONS** as logically following or logically not following an argument.

- **REVISION TIP** - Try to construct summary sheets that evaluate in this kind of way, by considering different definitions, the assumptions different philosophers make and the strength or otherwise of the argument that follows. Breaking it up this way forms a natural way of starting your essay. For example, in criticising Hume's view of miracles, we could say: "Hume's definition is inadequate, his assumptions restrictive and the conclusion he therefore comes to is invalid."

"To what extent" is used twice as a command phrase to begin the question. This invites the answer "to some extent" or "completely" or "not at all". For example, if we are asked to what extent God reveals himself through sacred writings, we will need to argue either that this is only one of several ways God reveals himself, or to say that it is the only way and as such a complete, final revelation of God, or that God doesn't reveal himself at all through sacred writings. "To what extent" also invites a consideration of what exactly it is about God we can see in the Bible: God's character, actions, view of humanity and creation, the things God hates and loves: these are all relevant and require practice in taking a line on a question.

How to Bring Specification and Past Questions Together

The specification gives an outline of the topics examined, and the subdivisions within the specification tell us which "twists" (as I call them) to expect. By lining up past questions against the specification we also get a clearer idea of how to interpret the specification, and hence this allows us to predict more accurately questions in the future.

In this chapter we will break the specification down into sub-units and then match questions to each subdivision. Possible future questions are indicated by a star, past questions already set by a tick.

Please note: We cannot reproduce May 2013 questions exactly, until ten months after the exam. I have given a general indication of the area examined in May 2013, and also in the table in the previous chapter I have indicated those areas examined in these two papers with a cross, so you can more easily spot the gaps. More gaps indicate higher probability, and now we combine this with the idea of "examining the twists" which have not been given yet to a question or a syllabus theme.

AS PHILOSOPHY OF RELIGION (OCR G571)

Plato: The Analogy of the Cave

▸ **The Republic VII. 514A-521B**

Candidates should be able to demonstrate knowledge and understanding of what might be represented in the Analogy of the Cave by the following:

▸ **The prisoners, the shadows, the cave itself, the outside world, the sun, the journey out of the cave and the return to the prisoners**

June 2009 (a & b)
- ✓ Explain the Analogy of the Cave in Plato's Republic
- ✓ "The Analogy of the Cave tells us nothing about reality." Discuss

Jan 2013 (a & b)
- ✓ Explain Plato's Analogy of the Cave
- ✓ "Plato is wrong to say that most people live in the shadow world." Discuss

Possible future question (Jan 2013 part a & b was similar to this)
- ★ Explain the meaning of the different elements in Plato's Analogy of the Cave
- ★ To what extent is the Analogy of the Cave a useful explanation of reality?

Plato: The concept of the forms; the form of the good

Candidates should understand what Plato meant by "Forms" and be able to demonstrate knowledge and understanding of:

▸ **The relationship between concepts and phenomena**

Possible future question (a & b)

★ Explain the relationship between concepts and phenomena in Plato's thought

★ "Plato's thought has useful things to teach us about reality." Discuss

▸ **The concept of "Ideals"**

Jan 2010 (a & b)

✓ Explain the concept of Ideals in Plato's writings

✓ "Ideals are an illusion; we can only experience what is real." Discuss

▸ **The relationship between the Form of the Good and the other Forms**

June 2012 (a & b)

✓ Explain the relationship between Plato's Form of the Good and other Forms

✓ "The Forms teach us nothing about the physical world." Discuss

Aristotle: Ideas about cause in purpose in relation to God (Metaphysics Book 12)

▶ **Aristotle's understanding of material, efficient, formal and final cause**

June 2009 (a & b)

✓ Explain what Aristotle meant by final cause
✓ To what extent does the concept of final cause teach us anything about the real world?

June 2011 (a & b)

✓ Asked a question about the four causes in Aristotle
✓ Required us to evaluate the four causes as a description of reality

The examiner commented of student answers to part b that "far too many candidates took little notice of the assumptions surrounding the notion of the final cause", and of part a noted that "too many students confuse Aristotle and Aquinas".

▶ **Aristotle's concept of the Prime Mover**

June 2012 (a & b)

✓ Explain Aristotle's concept of the Prime Mover
✓ "An accidental universe is as likely as a created one." Discuss

Note: The examiner makes this comment about Aristotle's empiricism on Q4b June 2012: "Many candidates argued that there was no physical evidence for the Forms, many attempted to describe the Third Man argument of Aristotle, though relatively few made use of any of his detailed, and rather simpler, criticisms in Nicomachean Ethics Book I, Chapter vi."

Judaeo-Christian influences on Philosophy of Religion

Candidates should be familiar with biblical texts to exemplify the topics below. There are no prescribed texts.

▸ **The concept of God as creator**

May 2013 (a & b)

✓ Asked us to explain "creatio ex nihilo"

✓ Asked us to discuss whether judgement was fair as he created us

▸ **The way the Bible presents God as involved with his creation**

Possible future question (a & b)

★ Explain what the Bible means by a Creator God involved with his creation

★ "The biblical account of God as Creator cannot be reconciled with scientific views of reality." Discuss

▸ **The imagery of God as a craftsman**

June 2010 (a & b)

✓ Compare the concept of God as Prime Mover with the idea of God as craftsman

✓ "Only philosophers can explain creation." Discuss

▶ The concepts of omnipotence, omniscience and omnipresence

Possible future question (a & b)

★ Explain how God's omnipotence can coexist with God's benevolence

★ If God knows everything, how can evil exist?

▶ The concept of "creatio ex nihilo"

Jan 2010 (a & b)

✓ Explain the concept of "creatio ex nihilo"

✓ "Nothing comes from nothing." Discuss

May 2013 (a & b)

✓ Asked us to explain "creatio ex nihilo"

✓ Asked us to discuss whether judgement was fair, as He created us

Compare this view with Aristotle's Prime Mover

Possible future question (a & b)

★ Compare and contrast Aristotle's idea of the Prime Mover with the idea of God as Creator in the Judaeo-Christian tradition

★ "God is involved with his Creation." Discuss

Possible part b question

★ "God who made the world is responsible for everything that happens." Discuss

The goodness of God

▸ **The ways in which the God of the Bible is seen as morally perfect and the source of human ethics**

Jan 2011 (a & b)

- ✓ Explain what it means to say that "God is good"
- ✓ To what extent are things only good because God commands them?

▸ **The concept of God as lawgiver and as judge**

Jan 2009 (a & b)

- ✓ Explain the Judaeo-Christian concept of God as law-giver and judge
- ✓ "God has no right to judge human beings." Discuss

▸ **Consider whether, in a biblical context, God commands things because they are good or whether things are good because God commands them**

Jan 2012 (a & b)

- ✓ Explain biblical beliefs about the attributes of God
- ✓ "The Bible is too inconsistent to be used for moral teachings." Discuss

Traditional arguments for the existence of God

▸ The ontological argument from Anselm and Descartes

June 2010 (a & b)

- ✓ Explain Anselm's ontological argument
- ✓ "It is pointless to deny the logical necessity of the existence of God." Discuss

May 2013 (a & b)

- ✓ Asked us to explain Descartes' ontological argument
- ✓ Required that we discuss whether his argument was valid

▸ Challenges to it from Gaunilo and Kant

Possible future question (a & b)

- ★ Explain how Kant challenged the ontological argument
- ★ To what extent was Kant successful in his criticisms of the ontological argument? Anselm's understanding of God - his understanding of the differences between contingent and necessary existence

Possible future question (a & b)

- ★ Explain Anselm's distinction between necessary and contingent existence
- ★ "Only God necessarily exists; everything else is contingent." Discuss

▸ **Descartes' understanding of existence as a perfection which God cannot lack**

Possible future question (a & b)

★ Explain Descartes' argument that perfection is an attribute of God

★ "Descartes' argument is ultimately unconvincing." Discuss

▸ **Gaunilo's analogy of the island in On Behalf of the Fool**

Possible future question (a & b)

★ Explain how Gaunilo's analogy of the island affects Anselm's ontological argument

★ "Gaunilo's analogy of the island is fatal to Anselm's argument." Discuss

The cosmological argument from Aquinas and Copleston;
challenges from Hume and Russell

▸ The cosmological argument from Aquinas and Copleston

June 2009 (a & b)

- ✓ Explain Aquinas' cosmological argument
- ✓ To what extent were Russell's criticisms of the cosmological argument successful?

▸ The arguments put forward by Copleston in the 1948 radio debate with Russell and Russell's counter arguments

Jan 2012 (a & b)

- ✓ Explain the arguments put forward by Copleston in his radio debate with Russell
- ✓ How far was Russell successful in countering Copleston's argument in the radio debate?

▸ Hume's criticisms of the cosmological argument

May 2011 (a & b)

- ✓ Explain Hume's criticisms of the cosmological argument
- ✓ To what extent was Hume successful in his critique of the cosmological argument?

The examiner commented on part a: "Some candidates were able to explain Hume's observation of the role of habit in linking cause to effect, which a few excellent answers were able to identify as the fallacy of affirmation of the consequent. Bertrand Russell was used regularly and to good effect as a development of Hume's ideas on infinite regress."

*The teleological argument from Aquinas and Paley;
challenges from Hume, Mill and Darwin*

▸ **The teleological argument from Aquinas and Paley**

June 2011 (a & b)

✓ Explain Paley's argument for the existence of God

✓ "The universe has no purpose". Discuss

Possible future question (a & b)

★ Explain Aquinas' argument for the existence of God

★ "Aquinas' argument is unconvincing." Discuss

▸ **The challenges to it from Hume, Mill and Darwinism**

Jan 2010 (a & b)

✓ Explain Mill's challenges to the teleological argument

✓ Evaluate the claim that the universe has too many flaws to be designed

Jan 2013 (a & b)

✓ Explain Mill's criticisms of the design argument

✓ "The teleological argument has successfully survived all criticisms." Discuss

Possible future question (a & b)

★ Explain how Darwinism challenges the teleological argument

★ "Darwin's challenges to the teleological argument are unconvincing." Discuss

The moral argument from Kant: psychological challenges from Freud

- **The moral argument from Kant, including his concept of the "summum bonum" and his inferences about innate moral awareness**

  June 2009 (a & b)

  ✓ Explain Kant's moral argument for the existence of God

  ✓ "Moral awareness has nothing to do with God." Discuss

  Possible future question (a & b)

  ★ Explain Kant's view that moral awareness is innate

  ★ "Moral awareness is a product of our upbringing." Discuss

  Jan 2011 (a & b)

  ✓ Explain what Kant means by "summum bonum"

  ✓ "The existence of morality is not evidence for the existence of God." Discuss

- **Psychological challenges from Freud to the moral argument, his view that moral awareness comes from sources other than God**

  June 2010 (a & b) and Jan 2013 (a & b) was very similar

  ✓ Explain Freud's view that moral awareness comes from sources other than God

  ✓ "God is the only explanation of moral awareness." Discuss

Challenges to religious belief: the problem of evil

▸ The problem of evil: the classic theodicies of Augustine and Irenaeus

June 2009 (a & b)

✓ Explain why Irenaeus argues that the existence of evil is a necessary part of the universe

✓ "Irenaeus is wrong: evil disproves the existence of God." Discuss

May 2011 (a & b)

✓ Explain the Irenaean theodicy

✓ To what extent can evil be said to be simply a test?

May 2013 (a & b)

✓ Asked us to explain Augustine's and Irenaeus' theodicy

✓ Asked us to discuss whether the presence of too much evil disproves God

The examiner commented on part a answers: "A number of candidates were able to make good use of the 'image'/'likeness' distinction found in Genesis 1:26. Better responses explored the way that virtues could be developed towards the likeness of God (in a much more Hickean way). It was pleasing to see some candidates identifying the link between the immaturity of Adam and Eve with Irenaeus' explanation of why man was not made perfect from the beginning through the analogy of a mother giving a child milk.

Possible future question (a & b)

★ Explain Augustinian theodicy

★ "Augustine fails to provide a convincing explanation for the existence of evil." Discuss

▸ **The nature of the problem of evil and the possible differences between natural and moral evil**

Jan 2011 (a & b)

✓ Explain the nature of the problem of evil

✓ "Moral evil may be the fault of humanity but natural evil is God's fault." Discuss

▸ **How each theodicy understands the responsibility of God for the existence of evil in the world**

Possible future question (a & b)

★ Explain how the theodicies of Augustine and Irenaeus understand God's responsibility for evil

★ "The existence of evil cannot be explained adequately by theodicy." Discuss

▸ **The origins of evil and the role of human free will**

Possible future question (a & b)

★ Explain the origins of evil

★ "Evil is purely a result of human free will." Discuss

Religion and science

▸ **Scientific and philosophical views on the creation of the universe; particularly the debate between Creationism and the Big Bang theory**

June 2009 (a & b)

- ✓ Explain the debate between Creationism and Big Bang theory
- ✓ "The Big Bang theory is more believable than Creationism." Discuss

Jan 2011 (a & b)

- ✓ Explain why some Creationists do not believe in Big Bang theory
- ✓ "Scientists are the only ones who can explain why the universe is here." Discuss

▸ **Darwinism and various developments of evolutionary theory**

Jan 2010 (a & b)

- ✓ Explain Darwinism and evolutionary theory
- ✓ "The universe is too complex for evolutionary theory to explain it." Discuss

Jan 2013 (a & b)

- ✓ Explain the theory of evolution
- ✓ "God is the only explanation for the existence of life." Discuss

▶ **"Intelligent design" and "irreducible complexity"**

June 2010 (a & b)

✓ Explain the concept of irreducible complexity

✓ "There is no evidence of intelligent design in the universe." Discuss

May 2013 (a & b)

✓ Asks us to explain what is meant by intelligent design

✓ Asks us to discuss whether intelligent design makes sense

▶ **Religious responses to challenges posed by scientific views**

Jan 2012 (a & b)

✓ Compare scientific and philosophical views on the creation of the universe

✓ Evaluate the view that science can only explain how and not why the universe exists

A2 PHILOSOPHY OF RELIGION (OCR G581)

In this section we relate past questions (with the date set) to the specification and then consider which areas have not been examined on before. Possible future questions are marked below.

Religious language

▸ **Religious language - uses and purpose**

▸ **The via negativa (Apophatic Way)**

Jan 2013

✓ To what extent is the via negativa the only way to talk about God?

Possible future question

★ Critically assess how the via negativa establishes the meaningfulness of religious language

▸ **The verification and falsification principles**

Jan 2012

✓ "The falsification principle presents no real challenge to religious belief." Discuss

Possible future question

★ "The verification principle presents a serious threat to religious belief." Discuss

▶ **Different views on the meaningfulness of religious language**

June 2011

✓ Critically assess the claim that religious language is meaningless

▶ **The uses of symbol, analogy and myth to express human understanding of God**

June 2010

✓ Evaluate the claim that analogy can successfully be used to express the human understanding of God

Jan 2011

✓ Critically compare the use of myth with the use of analogy to express the human understanding of God

June 2013

✓ Asks us to discuss whether symbolic language is the best way to talk about God

Possible future questions

★ Critically compare the use of analogy with the use of symbol to express the human understanding of God

★ "Myth is the only form of religious language that does justice to the nature of God." Discuss

▸ **The views of the Vienna Circle, AJ Ayer, Anthony Flew, Ludwig Wittgenstein and Paul Tillich on religious language**

Jan 2010

✓ Critically assess the views of Paul Tillich on religious language

May 2012

✓ Critically assess Wittgenstein's belief that language games allow religious statements to have meaning

Possible future questions

★ Critically assess Ayer's view that religious language is meaningless

★ Compare and evaluate Ayer's and Flew's views of the meaningfulness of religious language

★ Assess the strengths of Anthony Flew's views of religious language

★ To what extent can God be adequately revealed through sacred writings?

Religious experience

Candidates should be able to demonstrate knowledge and understanding of the following in relation to God and religious belief:

▸ **Arguments from religious experience from William James**

June 2010

✓ Critically assess, with reference to William James, the argument from religious experience

▸ **The aims and main conclusions drawn by William James in The Varieties of Religious Experience**

Jan 2013

✓ Critically assess the aims and conclusions of William James' The Varieties of Religious Experience

▸ **The following different forms of religious experience: visions, voices, "numinous" experience, conversion experience, corporate religious experience**

June 2011

✓ "Visions are not caused by God but can be explained by science." Discuss

Jan 2012

✓ "Corporate religious experiences prove the existence of God." Discuss

May 2012

✓ Conversion experiences are the strongest evidence for the existence of God

Possible future questions

★ Critically assess the role of numinous experiences in producing faith in God

★ "Visions are essentially subjective, so prove nothing regarding God's existence." Discuss

▶ The concept of revelation through sacred writings

Jan 2011

✓ To what extent can God reveal himself through sacred writings?

Note: The examiner comments on the question above (Jan 2011 Q1): "A disappointingly large number of candidates failed to understand the nature of propositional and non-propositional approaches, arguing that the first implied direct revelation (normally literal) and the latter indirect revelation. Neither definition is correct. Very many failed to recognise that in the life of believers, both aspects are frequently present."

Possible future questions

★ Critically assess different models of revelation through sacred writings within a religious tradition

★ "Sacred writings are inevitably culture-bound." Discuss

Miracle

A study of how God might interact with humanity, by looking at the concept of miracle.

▸ **Different definitions of miracle, including an understanding of Hume**

▸ **The biblical concept of miracle and the issues this raises about God's activity in the world**

Possible future question

★ Critically assess the biblical concept of miracle and the issues it raises about God's activity in the world

▸ **The concept of miracle, and criticisms made by Hume and Wiles**

Jan 2011

✓ Evaluate Hume's claim that miracles are the least likely of events

The examiner wrote of the answers to this question: "A surprising number thought - contrary to Hume's own account - that he claimed the laws of nature were fixed and unbreakable, with miracles impossible."

Jun 2013

✓ Asks us to evaluate Wiles' view on miracles.

Possible future question

★ Evaluate Wiles' claim that the absence of widespread miracles makes it improbable that God exists

▸ **The implications of the concept of miracle for the problem of evil**

Jan 2012

   ✓ Critically assess the view that the concept of miracle is inconsistent with a belief in a benevolent God

Possible future questions

   ★ "An all-powerful God would miraculously prevent all forms of natural evil." Discuss

   ★ "The lack of evidence for miracles proves that God cannot be benevolent." Discuss

▸ **Candidates should be able to discuss whether modern people can be expected to believe in miracles, and whether miracles suggest an arbitrary or partisan God**

Jan 2010

   ✓ "A belief in miracles leads to the concept of a God who favours some but not all of his creation." Discuss

Possible future questions

   ★ "A belief in the miraculous cannot be reconciled with a scientific worldview." Discuss

   ★ "A belief in miracles suggests a primitive worldview." Discuss

Nature of God

▸ **God as eternal, omniscient, omnipotent and omnibenevolent - and the philosophical problems arising from these concepts**

Jan 2010

✓ Critically assess the philosophical problems raised by belief that God is omniscient

May 2011

✓ Critically assess the problems for believers who say that God is omniscient

Jan 2012

✓ Assess the claim that the universe shows no evidence of the existence of God

June 2012

✓ Evaluate the philosophical problems raised by the belief that God is eternal

Jan 2013

✓ Critically assess the philosophical problems raised by belief in an omnibenevolent God

Possible future question

★ "God's omnipotence is not compatible with his omnibenevolence." Discuss

- **The views of Boethius in his discussion of eternity and God's foreknowledge in Book 5 of The Consolations of Philosophy**

  June 2010

  - ✓ "Boethius was successful in his argument that God rewards and punishes justly." Discuss

  June 2013

  - ✓ Asks us to consider whether Boethius proves that God is just

- **The question as to whether or not a good God should reward and punish**

  Possible future question

  - ★ "A good God would never punish sinners." Discuss

Life and death

- **Distinctions between body and soul, as expressed in the thinking of Plato, Aristotle, John Hick and Richard Dawkins**

  June 2010

  - ✓ Critically compare Aristotle's and Richard Dawkins' views on body and soul

  Possible future questions

  - ★ Critically compare John Hick's and Plato's views on body and soul

★ Critically compare Plato's and Aristotle's views on body and soul

▸ **Other concepts of the body/soul distinction**

May 2011

✓ Evaluate the claim that the soul is distinct from the body

Possible future question

★ "The body and soul are one entity." Discuss

▸ **Different views of life after death: resurrection and reincarnation**

Jan 2011

✓ "Resurrection is more likely to be true than reincarnation." Discuss

The examiner comments about this question: "It was disappointing that very few said anything about what was needed to be a continuous person, a question which for many philosophers is central to the plausibility of either theory of life after death."

Jan 2013

✓ "The concept of disembodied existence after death is incoherent." Discuss

Possible future question

★ Critically evaluate the view that human beings can be reincarnated

▸ **Questions surrounding the nature of disembodied existence**

Jan 2010

✓ Evaluate the claim that there can be no disembodied existence after death

✓ "Life after death cannot involve a physical form." Discuss

▸ **The relationship between the afterlife and the problem of evil**

June 2010

✓ To what extent is belief in an afterlife necessary for resolving problems raised by the existence of evil?

June 2013

✓ Asks us to consider whether evil can be justified without an afterlife

Possible future question

★ "The existence of an afterlife makes sense of an unjust world." Discuss

What the Examiner Says

Every year the examiner produces a report on student answers available on the OCR website. It is possible to extract from these general principles of what goes wrong when you write essays under exam conditions. Actually the same points are made over and over again, as if no one ever reads the reports, and if they do, they fail to learn from them. I have summarised here the main points the examiner makes, and then I suggest 12 things to practise to try and eliminate these errors.

AS PHILOSOPHY

Answer the question

It sounds an obvious point, but nearly every year the examiner complains that students are deviating from the question, either because they have learned a pre-prepared answer, or because they have more knowledge on another (perhaps related) area and so feel compelled to prove it.

Enormous efforts are made for little credit, as this comment in January 2011 indicates:

> "An examination at this level is not primarily a test of what candidates know, but rather of how well they can respond to the question. Some candidates wrote at enormous length, covering every theory they could remember, but often without demonstrating how these might be remotely relevant."

As another example, here's a comment praising relevance from a recent report:

> "Good candidates kept the question in mind throughout."
> (Jan 2012 AS Ethics Q4b)

You will not achieve an A grade if you don't answer the exact question set.

When you go into an exam, take a highlighter pen and highlight the key words and phrases. Hopefully, if you study this book carefully, you will understand what sort of command words (like "explain") to expect, and indeed, what kind of questions, as the examiner tends to repeat key phrases in different questions. A comment like the one below is fairly typical:

> "Generally, candidates fared well provided they answered the question which had been set and not the one they hoped would be set. Candidates need to be reminded to read the question and then answer the question." (June 2012)

▸ **Practise: making a reference to the question in every paragraph you write**

▸ **Know your key terms throughly**

In a previous chapter I listed the technical vocabulary in different areas of the syllabus. This creates a minimal list of technical terms you must understand and know. There is no excuse for entering an exam in a state of muddle over the distinction between a priori and a posteriori. Here are comments from recent examiner's reports.

"Words which seemed to have been ignored (or misunderstood) are 'universe', 'inconsistent' and 'biblical'." (Jan 2012 AS Philosophy) "Significant numbers seemed unaware that a predicate is part of a sentence and is not a quality of a thing." (June 2012 AS Philosophy)

Then in a longer extract, the examiner reiterates this point:

"Unfortunately, there are still candidates who attempt this examination with insecure knowledge of basic philosophical concepts and terminology. Many remain unaware of the correct meaning of terms such as 'empirical', 'logical', 'refute', 'metaphysical', 'a priori' or 'a posteriori'. Especially common errors were 'analytical' for 'analytic' - especially and 'scientifical' for 'scientific'. This subject presupposes familiarity with basic philosophical notions and some candidates have paid too little attention to these."

▸ **Practise: learning key definitions off by heart**

▸ **Reflect, don't just memorise**

"Some candidates appeared to have attempted to learn theories, leading to less successful responses: more able responses showed evidence of reflection on theories, with the best showing the benefits of original thought. It cannot be too often stressed that examiners - and the nature of the subject - expect candidates to demonstrate that they have considered and reflected on ideas and not merely learned them."
(AS Philosophy Jan 2012)

How do we "reflect on theories"? My argument in this book is that we reflect on theories by not just learning key points off by heart, but also by understanding (and being prepared to challenge) key **ASSUMPTIONS** the theory makes and reflecting carefully on the **WORLDVIEW** the theory comes out of. We then practise applying the key **PRINCIPLES** suggested by a theory to a particular issue (preferably using our own examples to ground the explanation).

▶ **Practise: reflective writing by peer group comparison and using examples of good practice on the PushMe Press website**

▶ **Show higher order skills**

> *"Despite good AO1 performance, AO2 skills were often lacking. It continues to be the characteristic of many candidates to believe that just because a number of philosophers have criticised a theory, it must be wrong, and when evaluating a question, you simply need to count the philosophers who make points on each side of the argument and see which side has more in it." (June 2012 examiner's report)*

What are these AO1 and AO2 skills? In general terms these "descriptors" as they are called can be expressed thus for AS and A2 (at A2 the whole essay is assessed according to these).

AO1 - In part a of AS questions you must select and demonstrate clearly relevant knowledge and understanding through the use of evidence, examples and correct language and terminology appropriate to Philosophy of Religion.

For top marks (25 of the 35 marks are awarded for AO1 criteria at AS, 21/35 at A2) you will need:

1. A very high level of ability to select and deploy relevant information

2. Accurate use of technical terms

3. A well-structured answer

AO2 - In part b of AS questions you must sustain a critical line of argument and justify a point of view.

For top marks (ten marks for AO2 criteria awarded out of 35 at AS, 14 marks awarded for these AO2 skills out of 35 at A2) you must:

1. Comprehend the demands of the question

2. Use a wide range of evidence

3. Show understanding and critical analysis of different viewpoints

▸ **Practise: reading the list of AO2 skills before you start your essay, and re-read after you've finished**

▸ **Argue, don't assert**

It's worth reflecting long and hard on the longer quotes from examiner's reports below:

> *"A statement of a viewpoint is not an argument, and argument by assertion is inappropriate in philosophical writing. Many responses simply presented alternative viewpoints but made no attempt to use these to work to their own conclusions. Candidates would benefit from thinking through the implications*

of the descriptors in the published levels of response used for marking - these are invaluable for explaining precisely those abilities rewarded by examiners." (Jan 2012 AS Philosophy of Religion)

"It is important that candidates engage with arguments: examiners seek evidence that views have been thoughtfully considered. A list of the arguments of different philosophers does not become a considered argument simply because 'however' is occasionally inserted into a narrative account." (June 2012 AS Philosophy of Religion)

"On occasions, some candidates, who were clearly very able, let themselves down by merely stating the views in detail and failing to deploy them as part of an overall argument." (June 2012 AS Philosophy of Religion Q1a)

"Some candidates struggled with the fundamental skill of constructing arguments, especially in part b of questions."

▸ **Practise: constructing arguments using the thesis - argument - conclusion model described in How to Write Philosophy Essays**

▸ **Illustrate with examples**

"Good marks were awarded for candidates who were able to demonstrate control of the material as well as being able to give examples from the biblical text to support their explanations." (June 2012 Q2a)

But make sure the examples are fresh and relevant. Some candidates continued to use dubious examples to support their explanations and many not even philosophical ones.

- **Practise: finding film extracts, news examples, or incidents in novels that illustrate ethical principles. Watch new films critically**

- **Produce an argument, not a list**

It is worth reflecting again on what constitutes an argument. If you have difficulty knowing how to practise forming an argument, I give plenty of examples in my book How to Write Philosophy Essays. Weaker candidates simply list points, rather than integrate them into a line of reasoning. A-grade candidates argue and explain points, showing how they link to assumptions and worldviews.

- **Practise: producing argument plans which sketch out counter-arguments and objections, like the Socratic method**

- **Be aware of the various issues (and applications) within a topic**

Here's a comment on how students handled Kant's moral argument. It shows how we are expected to take some modern scholars and bounce their views analytically off the arguments of more ancient scholars such as Anselm. one way of doing this is to produce a table with Anselm on one side and Plantinga on the other, and try to sequence Anselm's ideas down the table whilst then contrasting them with Plantinga's in the second column.

"The best answers, of which there were few, were able to use the work of Norman Malcolm or Alvin Plantinga to critically attack Kant's work through the notion of God's unlimited nature or maximal greatness to support Anselm's claim that God is a special case." (June 2012 AS Philosophy Q1b)

▸ **Practise: finding modern scholars who represent different viewpoints on old questions or theories**

▸ **Consult the PushMe Press website for extracts listed by section**

A2 PHILOSOPHY OF RELIGION

Th examiner's report of 2012 expressed disappointment particularly in the A2 Philosophy of Religion answers. "The overall standard of responses was slightly disappointing. Many answers were general in nature and failed to address the specific question set. A significant number of candidates seemed to be incapable of identifying which area of the specification was being assessed. It was not always that candidates' material was completely irrelevant; rather that the relevance was not made clear. Paragraphs on new thinkers or ideas would appear in many responses suddenly and without explanation".

▸ **Lack of knowledge of key terms affects quality of answers**

The examiner's report repeatedly makes the same point at A2 as at AS, that key terms are not properly understood. For example: "A particular problem for many was inadequate grasp of the grammar of philosophy, with terms such as 'prove' used as a synonym for 'argue'. Some would say of each thinker cited that he had 'proved' his view, even when it was controversial or opposed by other alleged 'proofs'; 'refute' used to mean 'deny'; 'a priori' often mistakenly used for 'innate'; 'a posteriori', 'analytic' and 'metaphysical' were commonly misunderstood. This is an examination in Philosophy of Religion, and understanding the conventions of the subject is as significant as understanding correct notation in Mathematics. Some candidates attempted, normally unsuccessfully, to answer philosophical questions with theological or scriptural assertions." (Jan 2012 A2 Philosophy of Religion).

- **Practise: writing full definitions of key terms on index cards and learn them**

- **Write critical analysis**

  "The best answers were able to analyse the experiences critically, giving a variety of examples. Successful analysis employed good use of psychological evidence such as 'mass hysteria' to challenge whether these experiences were even veridical or plausible at best. There was good use of Feuerbach, Freud, James and Swinburne as well as awareness of modern scientific research such as the 'God helmet'." (Jan 2012 A2 Philosophy of Religion Q1)

Sometimes the examiner praises high-quality candidates who go way beyond the syllabus with their analysis.

- **Practise: writing under timed conditions taking past questions (and looking at the mark schemes available on the OCR site) and then trying my possible future questions in Chapter 4**

- **Read the original sources**

Original sources are indicated in the specification. It is important to read these carefully and understand them for yourself, and not rely on textbook interpretations. One example is the radio debate between Copleston and Russell in the Philosophy of Religion specification.

"It was clear that few candidates had read the University Debate. Had the debate been read, many errors of understanding could have been avoided." (Jan 2012 A2 Philosophy of Religion Q4)

▸ **Practise: extracting your own quotes from original sources, and taking notes which map the arguments**

▸ **Don't tack your evaluation on at the end**

The examiner has encouraged us to separate analysis and evaluation at AS level (part a is always analysis and part b evaluation) and now we are criticised for tacking evaluation on at the end. The only way to learn how to integrate the two effectively is to read good examples and then try to copy their style. This comes with practice. How to construct such essays, and the language to use, is dealt with in my book with Brian Poxon How to Write Philosophy Essays (pushmepress.com, 2012).

▸ **Practise: taking a contrary position to a philosopher's view and producing summary sheets of strengths and weaknesses of different viewpoints**

Lightning Source UK Ltd.
Milton Keynes UK
UKOW05f1106240314

228702UK00002B/2/P